THE 100 MOST
ENCOURAGING VERSES
OF THE BIBLE

Books by Troy Schmidt

The 100 Best Bible Verses on Prayer
The 100 Best Bible Verses on Heaven
The 100 Most Encouraging Verses of the Bible

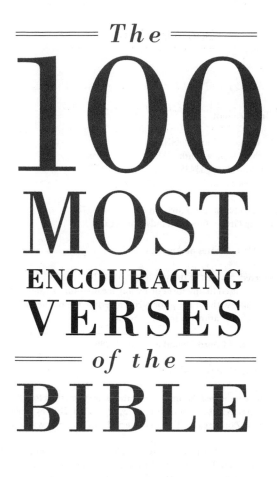

The
100
MOST
ENCOURAGING
VERSES
of the
BIBLE

TROY SCHMIDT

BETHANYHOUSE
a division of Baker Publishing Group
Minneapolis, Minnesota

© 2016 by Troy Schmidt

Published by Bethany House Publishers
11400 Hampshire Avenue South
Bloomington, Minnesota 55438
www.bethanyhouse.com

Bethany House Publishers is a division of
Baker Publishing Group, Grand Rapids, Michigan

Printed in the United States of America

Library of Congress Control Number: 2016942299

ISBN: 978-0-7642-1760-9

Cover design by Darren Welch Design

Author is represented by Working Title Agency

16 17 18 19 20 21 22   7 6 5 4 3 2 1

For Jim, Donna, and Tami

My dad, mom, and sister, who all battled cancer
and encouraged me by their strength

INTRODUCTION

We all get down at times. Sometimes it's our fault. Other times it's not.

No matter who we blame, it still hurts. We wonder if it will always be this way. Will the pain ever stop? Can a solution ever be found?

We see what others go through and we think, for a moment, that our situation is not that bad, but right now our situation is real and it hurts.

Thoughts go through our mind. Negative thoughts. Ungodly thoughts.

God doesn't love me any longer.

God doesn't care.

God can't do anything about my situation.

All not true. God loves you, He cares, and He can do something. Maybe not right now, but sometime . . . sooner or later.

In the meantime, He offers encouragement through His Word to calm our spirits struggling with doubt and worry.

God has been in the business of encouraging His people from the first sin in Genesis all the way to the last word in Revelation. He always offers truth from His perspective, usually by saying

"Trust me, I got this." There may be adjustments we need to make, but mostly we just need to stop worrying and give the outcome to God.

The key to all encouragement is trust in God.

Know He loves you.

Trust He cares.

Believe He's doing all He can.

These one hundred verses cover a wide range of encouragement God spoke throughout the Bible. They span a variety of situations experienced in over a thousand years of Bible history. Guess what . . . people then struggled and worried over the same things we struggle and worry about today.

So use these verses to bring encouragement to yourself and others. They are just words on the paper until you apply them to your life and know God is speaking directly to you.

Troy Schmidt
Windermere, FL
March 2015

1

GENESIS 9:16

Whenever the rainbow appears in the clouds, I will see it and remember the everlasting covenant between God and all living creatures of every kind on the earth.

After every torrential storm there's a rainbow.

Rainbows are caused by the reflection and refraction of water droplets illuminated by the sun, thereby creating a spectrum of light in the sky. Rainbows appear during the transition of rain to sun. After a dark and torrential storm, a rainbow is beautiful to look at.

God used this rainbow reminder to tell His people that He won't break a promise. The most devastating natural disaster had just occurred: the total and complete flooding of the earth, wiping out all human and animal life except for one relatively small remnant—Noah, his family, and the animals in the ark.

He promised Noah, and every descendant after him, that He would never do that again. As long as we see rainbows in the sky, we can know another flood like that won't strike again.

When we face devastating storms, we must remember that God's promises also shine like rainbows. God promises His love and mercy. Jesus promised to never leave us. He promised a place for us, where there is no crying or pain. The Holy Spirit is promised to intercede for us.

Those promises are beautiful to remember as we recover from the after-effects of our storms. Trust them. They are as evident and as real as a rainbow in the sky.

GENESIS 21:6

And Sarah said, "God has made me laugh, and all who hear will laugh with me." (NKJV)

There are many kinds of laughs. A polite laugh. A gentle snicker. A fake expression.

But a real gut-level, rib-hurting laugh, those are hard to come by.

A laugh is caused by a twisted surprise. You never expect a laugh. Someone does something unusual or strange or odd and you react with an emotional response that makes you feel good, forgetting your troubles for a moment.

Sarah learned she would have a child in old age: her eighties! That was a surprise. Unusual. Crazy! People her age should be retiring and settling in with the great-grandchildren. Yet she had never had a child in her life, and now God decided that she should become pregnant in her eighties.

That's hilarious.

In times of despair, God can do things to make you laugh. Sarah found the humor in her desperation. She had given up hope; now she offered up laughs.

Look for the laughter in your situation. Not a polite giggle or a fake "ha." Laugh at the unusual things God is doing and get ready for the uproarious surprises.

GENESIS 21:17

God heard the boy crying, and the angel of God called to Hagar from heaven and said to her, "What is the matter, Hagar? Do not be afraid; God has heard the boy crying as he lies there."

Hagar was a single mom, lost in the desert with her newborn son, Ishmael. Hagar had followed Sarah's orders and had sex with Abraham to give birth to a son, then gave up the child for adoption to her masters. After Isaac was born to Sarah and Abraham, Sarah didn't like Hagar's attitude and had Abraham send the other mother and child away.

Kicked out. Into the streets. The situation changed and their services were no longer needed. Hagar and Ishmael now wandered the desert, preparing to die, when an angel showed up and said God heard their cry.

If you're wandering right now, alone and hurting, God hears your cry, too. He knows where you are and what you are going through. God knows what happened and who is to blame, so you don't need to dwell on that. You have a need right now, like feeding your children or taking care of your physical needs.

God knows. And He's there. Hagar didn't even cry out for God. God heard the child's cries himself and He showed up. God doesn't need an invitation to help. He's already there.

You never wander alone.

GENESIS 22:17

I will surely bless you, and I will surely multiply your offspring as the stars of heaven and as the sand that is on the seashore. And your offspring shall possess the gate of his enemies. . . . (ESV)

I will surely bless you." Don't you love the assurance of that? Of course God will bless you. It's who He is.

Here, God spoke to Abraham. Abraham was faithful. He packed up and followed God wherever He said. Abraham did not withhold his son on the altar. Of course Abraham received blessing. But what about us?

God rewards faithfulness. Faithfulness leads to blessing. When you do everything God wants you to do, you receive a blessing. God wants to multiply that kind of faith inside you for generations to come. Seeing those generations multiply in numbers and faith is the greatest blessing to you and God.

As long as you are faithful, there is a blessing to be found. Not just one, but many more to come.

5

GENESIS 39:23

The warden paid no attention to anything under Joseph's care, because the Lord was with Joseph and gave him success in whatever he did.

Joseph, son of Jacob, was framed and sent to prison for a crime he didn't commit. End of his story? End of his life? No longer able to be used by God?

No way. God was just getting started with Joseph. Trapped in a place with no freedom, Joseph impressed the warden and interpreted dreams, catching the attention of Pharaoh. With four walls around him, Joseph could do things that changed the entire country and the course of history. In the worst of places, the best of things happened to him.

Success cannot be confined by circumstances. It is unleashed by those willing to be used by God wherever they are.

God is with those who are trapped. You may be in the worst of places, but God is still working. In a place of no freedom, you are free to work for God.

Don't let the walls define you or constrain you. Define your situation by what God can do where you are.

6

GENESIS 50:20

But as for you, you meant evil against me; but God meant it for good, in order to bring it about as it is this day, to save many people alive. (NKJV)

Joseph—separated from his family because of his brothers' jealousy, tossed in a pit, handed over to slave traders, sold as a slave, thrown into prison for years—looked back at it all years later and said, "It was all for good."

During that difficult time, God used Joseph to interpret a dream for Pharaoh and saved Egypt and many people from a serious famine. That pit stop and slave job were all steps in the process to save lives.

We need to look at the things that harm us and see them not for just the moment, but how they play out in the long run.

Joseph, lying in that pit, didn't think, *Wow, this is going to turn out great!*

Joseph, rotting in jail, didn't think, *I bet I'm going to save lots of lives.*

There is always purpose to the pain. What is that purpose? We probably don't know at the time. We must trust at the time that God will use this tragedy somehow.

EXODUS 2:25

So God looked on the Israelites and was concerned about them.

Nearly a million Israelite men, women, and children faced a life of slavery in Egypt. After four hundred years of living in the region, a new regime saw them as a threat and began to make their lives more and more difficult.

So they cried out.

God turned His attention to them, and His compassion for them grew. He wanted to help and began a process to save them from slavery.

God is looking down on you and is concerned about your situation. He heard your cry. If He was compassionate toward a million Israelites who were not the most appreciative and cooperative group, then why not you?

God's concern turns into action, initiating a rescue plan that could take weeks, months, or years to work. That may seem too long, but it's the perfect plan with the best outcome for the majority of people—but especially for you.

EXODUS 3:8

[A]nd I have come down to deliver them out of the hand
of the Egyptians and to bring them up out of that land
to a good and broad land, a land flowing with milk and
honey. . . . (ESV)

Usually we don't want to hear the words, "Don't make me
come down there," especially by an angry father hearing
his unruly kids downstairs creating havoc.

But in this case, we do want to hear our Father's voice saying,
"I'm coming down there," especially when we are in trouble
and need help ASAP.

God is willing to come down into our lives and intercede. He
wants to come with all His strength and all His reinforcements.
He will take matters into his own hands if we allow Him to. He
even wants to come with a plan to lead us out of our troubling
situation and into a delightful, bountiful paradise.

How do we know this? God came down and helped the Israelites in the Old Testament, escorting them out of slavery
in Egypt and to the Promised Land of milk and honey. In the
New Testament, Jesus came down, too. He actually walked
around in flesh and blood with a plan to die for our sins so we
can get out of a troubling, sinful death and enter a beautiful,
eternal paradise.

God has a rescue mission planned for you, too. Follow His
lead and allow Him to take you to a better place.

9

EXODUS 14:14

The Lord will fight for you; you need only to be still.

When there's a fight, the hardest thing to do is to remain still.

If you're threatened, you want to raise your fists and fight back. Your instinct puts you in a defensive position. All senses raised to DEFCON 1.

But when the Israelites went up against the Egyptians, rebelling and preparing to move out, God told them He'll take care of all the hard stuff. He'll take the punches and throw the punches. He'll fight . . . they should just stand off to the side.

The Lord will fight for you. Just don't move or get in the way. Don't try to step in and help Him. "I'll hold him, God, while you hit him in the stomach." He doesn't need you, frankly. You'll just get hurt in the process.

Whatever fight that's going on in your life, step back and let God take it on for you.

Be still and watch. You have ringside seats.

EXODUS 14:19–20

> And the Angel of God, who went before the camp of Israel, moved and went behind them; and the pillar of cloud went from before them and stood behind them. So it came between the camp of the Egyptians and the camp of Israel. Thus it was a cloud and darkness to the one, and it gave light by night to the other, so that the one did not come near the other all that night. (NKJV)

Wouldn't you have loved to see that pillar rising up between Israel and the enemies? How reassuring that must have been to the Israelites to see God physically stand between them and their problem.

That pillar still exists today in your life—you just can't see it.

God erects a barrier between you and your enemies in the spiritual realm. If you are one of His people, then you are on God's side and the enemies can't cross over unless He allows them to.

In the meantime, God brings light to His people, illuminating His love and power, our weakness and strength, the problem and the solution. While we see things clearly, the enemy scrambles around in darkness.

While it would be nice to have a visible pillar follow us around all the time, reassuring us, remember the Israelites saw this pillar and still doubted God's ability to provide—and rebelled frequently against Him.

Trusting and believing in His protection is more important than actually seeing it.

11

EXODUS 34:6–7

And he passed in front of Moses, proclaiming, "The Lord, the Lord, the compassionate and gracious God, slow to anger, abounding in love and faithfulness, maintaining love to thousands, and forgiving wickedness, rebellion and sin."

Remember these seven qualities of God as you go through life.

Compassionate—His heart breaks for your situation. He understands what it's like.

Gracious—He feels empathy for you and extends His help, even though, as a sinner, you don't deserve it.

Slow to anger—It takes a lot to get God mad.

Love—He loves with a sacrificial love, not a feeling of love that can change overnight or a conditional love based on your behavior.

Faithfulness—He stays true to you and focused on you, never giving up.

Maintaining—God does what He can to keep your relationship with Him running smoothly.

Forgiving—God forgives your sin, and you can know you are forgiven when you just ask.

Seven powerful qualities of God you can trust in. Why would you ever stray from or deny a God like this?

NUMBERS 6:24–26

The Lord bless you
and keep you;
the Lord make his face shine on you
and be gracious to you;
the Lord turn his face toward you
and give you peace.

The Lord told Moses to tell the priests to bless the Israelites this way. What a blessing for someone to receive. Asking the Lord to bring you joy. Asking the Lord to keep you close to His heart. Asking the Lord to smile favorably on your life. Asking the Lord to show grace when you mess up. Asking the Lord to pay attention to your needs. Asking the Lord to grant peace in the midst of chaos. Receive this blessing and know it's yours.

13

The Lord answered Moses, "Is the Lord's arm too short? Now you will see whether or not what I say will come true for you."

God's arms are not too short to help you.

Do you need to grab something out of your reach? God can give you a boost or take it off the top shelf and bring it to you.

Do you need a hug, feeling the warm embrace of God's arms around you? God's right there waiting.

Do you need a hand because you've fallen and can't get up? God extends His helping hand of grace.

Do you need some elbow room, feeling crowded with problems and overwhelmed? God can do that, too.

It's our arms that are too short to reach God. We can jump and jump with all our might, but we'll never reach God unless He reaches down to us.

Once His arms are there, they won't let go.

2 KINGS 6:17

> Then Elisha prayed and said, "O Lord, please open his eyes that he may see." So the Lord opened the eyes of the young man, and he saw, and behold, the mountain was full of horses and chariots of fire all around Elisha. (ESV)

If our eyes could only see the armies of angels all around us. Of course we feel all alone on the battlefield—all we see is ourselves.

We see our debt, our unemployment, our foreclosure, the mockers, the haters, the betrayers, the war of enemies. We can see our problem clearly in the bank statements, on the Internet, or those on the phone with us right now telling us all the things we've done wrong.

But unseen by us, fighting in another realm, is the army of God. Those angels battle the demons and their weapons of temptation, depression, doubt, guilt, and pessimism. They put up the barriers when needed and prevent any more harm from happening to us.

If we saw them, we'd be like, "Oh, bring it on, world!" We can still say that, but we'll have to accept that fact by faith, not sight.

15

2 CHRONICLES 20:15

[A]nd he said, "Listen, all Judah and the inhabitants of Jerusalem and King Jehoshaphat: thus says the Lord to you, 'Do not fear or be dismayed because of this great multitude, for the battle is not yours but God's.'" (NASB)

Whose battle are you fighting?

If you caused the problem and you're trying to find the resolution on your own, it's your battle.

If someone else caused the problem and you're trying to find the resolution on your own, it's your battle.

However, if you or someone else caused the problem and you're trusting God will find the resolution according to His will, it is God's battle. Once you turn it over to Him, realizing you're powerless in this fight, He accepts the responsibility for the outcome.

Since you've given it to Him, then any resolution is His resolution. You need not fear the outcome or be discouraged. You may not get what you want, but you trust this is what God wants.

So retreat and let God take it from here. You're not giving up. You're only trusting that God is a much better fighter than you are.

2 CHRONICLES 32:7–8

"Be strong and courageous, do not fear or be dismayed because of the king of Assyria nor because of all the horde that is with him; for the one with us is greater than the one with him. With him is only an arm of flesh, but with us is the Lord our God to help us and to fight our battles." And the people relied on the words of Hezekiah king of Judah. (NASB)

Hezekiah, sensing the people's fear of Assyria knocking on their border, said to them, "Be strong and courageous." Easier said than done. The king even reminded them that the enemy had a *vast* army. Choose your words carefully, Hezekiah. Did you have to say they had a vast army?

But Hezekiah wisely asked the people to consider this thought: who had the greater power on their side? The king of Assyria had an arm of flesh. Mildly impressive and maybe a bit frightening if there was a sword in that hand.

But the Israelites had God, whose arms can't be lopped off with a well-placed sword. God, who could not tire and doesn't need sleep. God, who could see everything and know every weakness. God, who fought for them before and would certainly fight for them again.

This representation of God inspired confidence in the people. It's not a physical battle. It's a spiritual battle. And if that's the case, God always wins.

So be strong and courageous because God is on your side.

JOB 2:3

The Lord said to Satan, "Have you considered My servant Job? For there is no one like him on the earth, a blameless and upright man fearing God and turning away from evil. And he still holds fast his integrity, although you incited Me against him to ruin him without cause." (NASB)

God is willing to bet on you.

Job was a righteous man, and God knew he would defy any attacks by Satan. He was confident Job wouldn't drop his faith or curse his Maker. So God allowed Satan to give Job his best shot. Job praised God throughout his ordeal.

God knows your deeds, your limits, and your strengths. He knows what Satan is doing to you. Maybe He's allowing your situation to play out just to show Satan that you're one of the good ones. He's confident you won't waver.

God wants to brag about you around others, tell your story in His book, watch you hold the trophy of victory at the end of the race.

So don't succumb to the temptation to hate or get angry at God.

Defy the odds and beat Satan at his own game.

JOB 2:6

So the Lord said to Satan, "Behold, he is in your power, only spare his life." (NASB)

When God made His bet with Satan over Job, Satan was not free to do whatever he pleased. God established the rules. He never asked Satan if he was okay the rules. God made the rules and Satan abided by them. The first time God allowed Satan access to Job, the physical body was off limits. The second time God allowed Satan access to Job's physical body, he could not push Job to death.

Satan is never completely in control. He must always follow the rules established by God. Satan is not all powerful.

Is the devil pestering you? Maybe, but God knows about your situation and even allows it. Sound cruel? If God allows Satan's influence on you, then your hardship must have a purpose. Maybe one day it'll be a story like Job's that someone will read, and it will give them hope. Maybe it's meant to increase your faith. Maybe, as a result of your situation, someone will accept Jesus Christ as their savior.

At that point, you will look back and understand why it was all worth it.

19

JOB 2:13

Then they sat on the ground with him for seven days and seven nights. No one said a word to him, because they saw how great his suffering was.

How encouraging to have friends willing to hang out with you during your darkest times. It's in those hard times that we find out who our friends really are.

Job's friends sat with him, denying their comfort by sitting in the dirt and sacrificing their time for seven days and nights. They didn't just stop by. They set up camp for their friend. Now, let's be honest, the friends did a terrible job encouraging Job when they opened their mouths, but they did much more for him by just sitting around and being with him.

We think we have to sit with our grieving friend to give advice and point out failures. The suffering person knows what they did and how they got to this place. All we can do, at times like these, is just be there.

Who is always there for you when you need them? Who is willing to just sit and experience the grief with you?

Many people don't have those kinds of friendships. Why? Maybe you aren't that kind of friend others need right now. Maybe now you can comfort others, and someday they can return the favor.

JOB 6:8–9

Oh, that I might have my request,
  that God would grant what I hope for,
that God would be willing to crush me,
  to let loose his hand and cut off my life!

Good thing God does not answer all our prayers, especially when things get so bad that we want to die.

Job reached that point. Everything (almost everything) was gone from his life. He thought it would be better if he never lived. That, he felt, would have spared all this trouble.

God knew the trouble wouldn't last forever. This was only temporary. Job thought the pain was forever. It wasn't. Soon Job's fortunes and life were restored twofold, twice as good as it was before.

If God had granted Job's request to die, Job would have missed this double blessing.

Job only needed a little encouragement in the meantime. He met with friends and he met with God. In the end, the pain passed.

Cry out to God if you must—be honest—but know there's a blessing of restoration around the corner. You don't want to miss it.

JOB 16:20–21

My intercessor is my friend
   as my eyes pour out tears to God;
on behalf of a man he pleads with God
   as one pleads for a friend.

Job cried out with the understanding that he was not alone in his situation.

He knew that God interceded for him, like a friend.

While we are trained to see God as King, Creator, and Conqueror, we can also see Him as a friendly ally. Yes, He's all of those other things—the titles still apply—but that doesn't mean He can't have all the qualities that we look for in a friend: someone who relates to us, who understands us, who laughs at our jokes, who hangs out with us, who we turn to in hard times.

It should be encouraging to know that God is your all-knowing, ever-present friend, who is always available to listen and ready to help.

PSALM 10:17–18

You, Lord, hear the desire of the afflicted;
  you encourage them, and you listen to their cry,
defending the fatherless and the oppressed,
  so that mere earthly mortals
  will never again strike terror.

Don't you love to root for the underdogs?
That team nobody expects to win? That person who didn't have all the training, expertise, or finances to succeed and yet, somehow, pulls it out in the end?

People flock to movies and read books about these kind of underdogs all the time.

God loves underdogs, too. He defends the fatherless and oppressed. Being an earthly mortal makes us all underdogs, and yet there are some on earth who live more stressed, less blessed, and less supported than others.

The fatherless never choose to be without a father. God steps in and says, "I'll be your Father."

The oppressed don't want to be oppressed. God steps in and says, "I'll defend you."

The afflicted hate their affliction. God steps in and says, "I'll heal you."

Underdogs, God is on your side and He's rooting for you.

PSALM 23:4

Even though I walk
   through the darkest valley,
I will fear no evil,
   for you are with me;
your rod and your staff,
   they comfort me.

God is heavily armed and following you wherever you go. Enemies in the shadows . . . God sees them.

Your vulnerable spots . . . God's got your blind side.

Walking through a dark time in your life . . . God shines brightly.

The words *even though* start this verse.

Even though darkness has inundated your life . . . *even though* you've made some disturbing choices . . . *even though* you're hanging out with the wrong crowd . . . *even though* your enemies want to see you go down and suffer . . . *even though* the world's falling apart . . .

God is there. No "even though" takes God by surprise or renders Him incapable. No "even though" separates you so far from God He can't find you.

God has all the tools He needs to keep His children safe.

PSALM 27:1

> The Lord is my light and my salvation;
> Whom shall I fear?
> The Lord is the defense of my life;
> Whom shall I dread? (NASB)

So why are you afraid?

God provides the light to see clearly where you are going and to scare away those enemies in the shadows who fear illumination.

God gives life eternal, saving you from death, rescuing you from the grave.

God is the ultimate stronghold, his power and strength revealed in His creation and His dominance over the devil and demons.

Light. Life. Strength.

Who else can protect you? What else do you need? Where on earth can you possibly be defenseless? When are you going to start trusting God and using His resources to take away your fear? It's all there for you and surrounding you.

Fear not. Trust Him.

PSALM 27:14

Wait for the Lord;
Be strong and let your heart take courage;
Yes, wait for the Lord. (NASB)

The waiting is the hardest part.

It's easy to say that God is real and that He loves His people. Many know for a fact that Jesus Christ died for them, and that by having a relationship with Him they will live with Him for eternity.

But the hardest struggle people have with God while on earth is the wait. Waiting for medical news. Waiting for a job status. Waiting for a relationship to get better. Waiting to hear from a prodigal child.

During that wait, doubt sneaks in and all kinds of discouraging things go through someone's mind, creating distrust between a person and God—things like *God doesn't care* or *God has forgotten me*. Those doubts run counter to the facts that we know about God (that He loves us and died for us), and yet, while waiting, all we know or we thought we knew can dissolve away.

This verse says "be strong." Hold on tightly to what you know for sure while waiting and never doubt. Take heart and continue to love God. Know that waiting doesn't mean God has forgotten you and stopped loving you. Know that waiting means He's working for you and preparing an answer for you. It's just not right now . . . but it's coming.

PSALM 46:1

God is our refuge and strength,
an ever-present help in trouble.

God is ever-present. He's always there when you need help.
If you're in trouble, He will see you through it.
If you need protection, His arms are always open.
If you feel weak, God flexes His muscles.

Why don't people feel God's presence when trouble hits? Instead, they feel that since a problem stands in front of them, God must be absent or weak.

God stays with you during the trouble. Sometimes He may remove the trouble, but most times He gives you what you really need during that time—protection, strength, and help that keeps trouble from becoming more troubling.

Our response should be to accept and know that God is there. Trust, relax, and lean against Him. He's ever-present and ever-ready to help you.

PSALM 91:11–12

For He shall give His angels charge over you,
To keep you in all your ways.
In their hands they shall bear you up,
Lest you dash your foot against a stone. (NKJV)

The term *guardian angel* never appears in the Bible, but at times we see glimpses of such things.

Some people believe there are angels assigned directly to us, a thought planted in us by movies like *It's a Wonderful Life*. It's nice to think that, but nowhere in the Bible do we see that one angel is assigned to us for our entire life.

However, we do see that God specifically commands angels to watch over us and protect us from slips, falls, and head-on collisions.

Would you rather have one angel keeping his eye on you or a whole battalion? This verse uses the plural to describe angels watching over us. The plural is much better.

So be comforted: God sends His angels to guard us, lift us up, push us out of the way, and help us up after falling.

They are His angels, not ours, and He has a lot of them.

PSALM 121:7–8

The Lord will keep you from all harm—
he will watch over your life;
the Lord will watch over your coming and going
both now and forevermore.

This verse can't be true, can it? God cannot keep us from *all* harm, because people get into car accidents all the time. Doctors give bad news. Robberies occur. Spouses walk out. Is God not doing His job, or is He incapable of defending against evil?

Psalm 121:7–8 comforts us by letting us know that God protects us from harm we may not know about. How many car accidents did God shield us from, and how many medical issues did He quietly heal? How many crimes were sidetracked or relationships soothed before they ever collapsed? The number would be staggering if we knew.

Yet we do not live in a perfect world at all. If it were perfect we would never want to leave. Bad things have to happen or God would not need to save us from this world.

God does a great job keeping us from harm here on earth, but ultimately the job will be completed in heaven where nothing will hurt us ever again.

PSALM 139:2–3

You know when I sit down and when I rise up;
  you discern my thoughts from afar.
You search out my path and my lying down
  and are acquainted with all my ways. (ESV)

God knows every step you took and every nap you slept (even if you were just resting your eyes).

He knows what you had for breakfast today (which you'll probably forget by four o'clock) and what you'll have for breakfast tomorrow.

God listens to your conversations and taps into your thoughts.

Basically, God provides around-the-clock watch.

For some, that's great news. "God pays attention to everything I do!"

For some, that's bad news. "God pays attention to everything I do?"

Whatever you do, know that you aren't forgotten. God isn't only watching the most popular celebrities. He's watching the ordinary and everyday people. Us.

God watches because He's interested and He cares. So what does He see?

PSALM 145:18

The Lord is near to all who call on him,
to all who call on him in truth. (ESV)

A hotline is a phone that directly dials to only one other place. If you picked up the phone on one end, it rang only on the other.

The hotline is never tied up or busy.

God has a hotline to all of us. When we pick up the prayer phone, it goes straight to God, not to His assistant or some intern studying to be God someday. Right to God.

If you try to call God through another means—fortune-tellers, psychics, or tarot cards—then the call gets corrupted because He was not called in truth.

The crystal-clear call to God knows that He hears all who call, takes your call despite your sin, and answers all prayers with *yes*, *no*, or *hold, please*.

So make the call in truth. The Lord will pick up and you'll have His undivided attention.

PSALM 147:3

He heals the brokenhearted
and binds up their wounds.

God always carries with Him glue and antiseptic.
God can reassemble and patch up the most broken
and shattered hearts and people on the planet. No job
is too hard.

God can also clean up and purify the dirtiest, most disgust-
ing lives wallowing in the filth of sin.

God is in the restoration business.

Others would throw away anything broken and filthy, finding
it difficult to look at or be around. They don't want to invest
the time and energy in making it new. So they toss it.

God takes the discarded lives, gluing them back together
with the Holy Spirit and cleaning out the infections with His
word. He makes the life better than it was!

So if you're broken down and covered with sin, don't worry,
God's ready to fix you up.

PROVERBS 3:5–6

Trust in the Lord with all your heart and lean not on your own understanding; in all your ways submit to him, and he will make your paths straight.

Trust does not meander or wander aimlessly.

Trust runs right at the issue, straight to the heart.

Trust does not try to lean on itself or on flimsy theories.

Trust leans on solid, proven, experienced facts.

Trust is not so-so or halfhearted. It does not rely on feelings.

Trust knows for sure, without a doubt, and is fully convinced.

Trust is not hearsay, just words from the mouth.

Trust is revealed in actions, throwing yourself fully in, diving headfirst, without using a net.

Whatever you're going through, trust in God with all you've got.

Leave no room for worry in your life.

PROVERBS 18:10

The name of the Lord is a fortified tower; the righteous run to it and are safe.

A tower in ancient times told people as they approached the city that this location was secure. It meant the city had resources, money, and military. Towers could allow people to see enemies off in the distance. When an enemy was upon them, the tower gave them a height advantage so they could shoot down on them and see the enemies' weaknesses from their vantage point.

A tower was built securely to keep from falling. Normally the tower was part of the wall surrounding the city, so it had a secure base.

Today, as we're faced with enemies and difficulties, we can run for the tower. God is our tower. He can see the problems ahead, understand the strategies for victory, and rest in a foundation that won't topple.

The verse says the "righteous" run to it—those who are right with God and already belong to His kingdom. If you're one of God's people and you're under attack, you have a secure shelter.

Run to it and be protected.

ISAIAH 40:31

But those who hope in the Lord
will renew their strength.

You probably worked out today. Or not.

At least, you probably wanted to work out today. Walk, run, lift a few weights . . . Why do we want to workout? We like strength. We like to feel confident and strong.

Physical strength gives us confidence. We walk a little straighter. We address problems more boldly.

In the spiritual world, it's not muscles that give us strength. It's hope.

Hope is strength.

If we lose hope, we lose confidence. We wobble, unsure and unsteady.

That hope cannot be in ourselves, because remember: We are weak. That hope needs to be in something stronger than us, outside of ourselves.

That hope must be in the Lord—confident and assured that He is in charge and that He will take care of us. He knows best, so we must be patient. He knows best, so we need not worry.

Get a workout today and flex your muscle by putting all your hope in God. Feeling stronger already?

ISAIAH 41:10

So do not fear, for I am with you;
　　do not be dismayed, for I am your God.
I will strengthen you and help you;
　　I will uphold you with my righteous right hand.

What causes fear and worry in our lives? What causes weakness and unsteadiness?

Being alone.

The feeling of loneliness—that it's just us versus the world—causes all our fears and worries. We know we can't do it alone. We know we are helpless when we see the forces rise up against us.

So what can take away our loneliness that causes our fear and worry? Relationship.

Knowing that someone is there for us, watching our backs, picking us up when we stumble, fighting off the attackers, protecting us from harm.

God promises to be there with us. We don't have to be dismayed unless we refuse His companionship. He's right there reaching out His hand. Take it and fear no more.

JEREMIAH 29:11

"For I know the plans I have for you," declares the Lord, "plans to prosper you and not to harm you, plans to give you hope and a future."

God has plans for you. If you saw them right now, you'd probably freak. "He wants me to do what?!" You would feel unprepared.

Right now God is preparing you for those plans. Sometimes there are good things in those plans. Sometimes there are bad things. Both have a purpose and a path to get you where you need to go. Plans to shape you, challenge you, grow you, and strengthen you.

All of God's plans lead to prosperity. Not financial, necessarily, but always spiritual. He can use you to bring unity where there is division, hope where there is hopelessness, love where there is hate, wisdom where there is foolishness. Plans that would prosper not only yourself, but all those around you.

So don't follow your plans—follow God's plans. Whatever happens in your life, make it a part of the plan to grow through it and discover God's will.

That's the best plan for your future.

JEREMIAH 30:11

"I am with you and will save you,"
declares the Lord.
"Though I completely destroy all the nations
among which I scatter you,
I will not completely destroy you.
I will discipline you but only in due measure;
I will not let you go entirely unpunished."

Sometimes God has to spank us. We may be injured but never destroyed. We may be scattered but not completely lost.

He only gives us a measure—say, an eighth of a teaspoon—of the full pounding that we deserve. The wages of sin is death, but God only slaps our wrist thanks to His grace.

God cannot leave us undisciplined or He would be promoting unjust behavior.

God's heart is to save us. The discipline is for our good. The discipline saves our lives.

When going through hard times, ask yourself if this is a trial (life happens), a tribulation (enemies attack), or a discipline (God punishment).

Discipline and punishment lead us to salvation or a better understanding of truth.

Accept the discipline and allow it to save you.

HABAKKUK 3:19

The Sovereign Lord is my strength;
he makes my feet like the feet of a deer,
he enables me to tread on the heights.

What's the highest you've ever reached? The tallest building you've ever ascended? The greatest mountain you've ever scaled?

God wants you to go higher.

God helps you reach new heights. As a child, we wanted to grab things on the top shelf or see over the crowds or climb to the top of the stairs. We did not like being so small.

We needed a boost, so our parents grabbed us and helped us up. We reached new heights, but only with Mom or Dad's help.

God wants your marriage to be the absolute best. He wants your job to exceed all expectations.

God wants to answer your impossible dreams. You can't get there on your own strength. But you can get there with God's strength. He wants to give you a boost.

39

ZEPHANIAH 3:20

"At that time I will gather you;
at that time I will bring you home.
I will give you honor and praise
among all the peoples of the earth
when I restore your fortunes
before your very eyes,"
says the Lord.

A hero's welcome.

We love to honor those heroes when they return home with cheers and music, clapping and ticker tape. The heroes wave from their vehicles as they parade down the streets.

When we've been away from God and decide to return to Him, there's a celebration then, too. It may not happen on earth. Earth does not always celebrate prodigals. But heaven does.

Heaven loves to hear breaking news.

"Another wayward child of God has returned home. We go to our correspondent Gabriel standing by live on Earth. Gabe . . ." You get the idea.

Angels glued to the news, hearing every word, then cries of praise to God for never giving up, showing mercy to the lost.

God wants to restore our lost fortunes. It may be here on earth or it may be in heaven, where our treasures need to be stored. Either way, a hero's welcome is awaiting you if you stay faithful and return home where you belong.

ZECHARIAH 4:6

"Not by might nor by power, but by my Spirit," says the
Lord Almighty.

How are things going to get done in your life? By your
strength? By your power?

You may be able to bench-press 250 pounds, but
circumstances of life are not going to happen by your own
strength. No, it's God's spirit who makes things happen.

It's frustrating to work and work, pushing your agenda and
focusing on your dreams only to see it all collapse. You've given
so much and sacrificed it all. Now what do you have to show
for it?

Here's a new tactic. Let God do the heavy lifting. He can
bench-press far more. He has more stamina. And He knows
right where to move the heavy pieces without wasting a lot of
time.

Take a rest and let His Spirit take it from here. You'll feel
much better.

MATTHEW 5:4

Blessed are those who mourn,
For they shall be comforted.

Mourning is a blessing?

Not exactly, but you can be blessed when you mourn, meaning you can find happiness while you grieve. Our sadness can turn to joy if we turn to God.

We can't find happiness in death if we look to the earth for help. The world can only say things like, "He's in a better place," or "We'll all die one day," or "At least she's not suffering." But do we really know they are in a better place, and is there no suffering where they are? Also, how does that help us face life without that person or encourage us about our own death?

Mourning turns to blessing when we know that Jesus Christ died for our sins and that those sins no longer separate us from God. Our slate is wiped clean and all charges are dropped. Jesus paid the price for our sins, and His death became our death.

We are separated from earth and our loved ones, but only for a time. Heaven becomes a reunion of all believers focusing everything on one God. What a blessing that will be.

Those standing before God aren't even thinking about mourning. They are praising Him! That should comfort you and bless you.

MATTHEW 5:10

Blessed are those who are persecuted for
righteousness' sake,
For theirs is the kingdom of heaven.

Persecution is a blessing?

Once again, not exactly. Persecution hurts when your character, life, and beliefs are scrutinized and mocked. Persecution is pain, the torture of body, the destruction of homes, and the massacre of loved ones.

Where's the happiness in that?

The only blessing that can occur from persecution is that it leads you to heaven. God appreciates, rewards, and anticipates the arrival of those persecuted for their faith in Jesus Christ. God shows gratitude to people who left homes and said good-bye to people for His sake.

They get an extra share of thanks from God himself.

Persecution is horrible, but not unexpected. It's been happening for two thousand years on earth and will continue until the very last second, when Jesus returns. For a believer, persecution does not end their life. It begins a glorious homecoming to a God who deeply appreciates them for staying righteous.

MATTHEW 6:25

Therefore I say to you, do not worry about your life, what you will eat or what you will drink; nor about your body, what you will put on. Is not life more than food and the body more than clothing? (NKJV)

Well if Jesus said not to worry, then we won't. Right? So if God said we don't have to worry about things, why do we? Paycheck runs short . . . we turn to worry. Pink slip handed . . . we run to worry. Diagnosis revealed . . . full-on sprint to worry.

Worry is like our comfort zone when things go bad, and yet it offers no comfort at all. We worry because the world says it's acceptable to worry. Everyone else worries, so why not you? Yet worry is not a solution. It's a trap we fall into and can't get out of.

Worry occurs when we see no earthly solution to our situation. In that sense, worry speaks the truth—sometimes there aren't any earthly solutions. So instead of worrying, turn to the heavenly solution.

Turn to God and allow Him to provide the basic necessities of living—food, drink, and clothes. Jesus promised to help. All you have to do is trust.

MATTHEW 6:33

But seek first the kingdom of God and His righteousness, and all these things shall be added to you. (NKJV)

When everything around you collapses, sputters, or dies, where do you turn? What will you do?

This verse tells you to seek. Begin a journey of discovery, finding the eternal in a world of the temporary.

Seek His kingdom. What is that? Find out where God is working. Go to the places God has set up His camp. Get involved in church. Serve. Help others. Spread the Good News.

Seek His righteousness. Become more godly in your heart. Read the Word. Exhibit the fruits of the Spirit. Think the right thoughts. Avoid negativity in people and media. Be pure and righteous.

Seek the inward (His righteousness) and the outward (His kingdom), and the promise of this verse says He will give you all the things you need. What are those things? What was earlier mentioned in Matthew 6—food, drink, clothes. Seek God and He'll provide.

MATTHEW 6:34

Therefore do not worry about tomorrow, for tomorrow will worry about itself. Each day has enough trouble of its own.

Does any good come out of worry? Not unless you're a doctor. Worry and stress cause physical damage to people and increase a doctor's clientele. Everything from lack of sleep to depression to rashes can be linked to worry and fill up a doctor's schedule.

Worry does no good. Nothing. Worry doesn't change the problem. Worry only magnifies the problem, making it bigger than it really is. Worry does nothing about today or tomorrow—it only makes you have a bad day and look forward to another bad day.

Jesus told His disciples to stop worrying, especially about tomorrow. Focus on today and get the things done that you need to get done, and stop worrying about what you think might happen. We all have enough on our plate today.

This means we need to trust God with tomorrow while we do what we need to do today.

We can't escape troubles and problems, but we can avoid worry. That is one thing we do have control over.

MATTHEW 7:11

If you then, being evil, know how to give good gifts to your children, how much more will your Father who is in heaven give good things to those who ask Him! (NKJV)

God loves to give gifts to His children. It's the same feeling a parent has at Christmas or a birthday, as a child sees all the presents and rips into them with glee. We like to make our children happy. So does God.

God has gifts to give you. You may want a new car or a new house or a new job, and God may have that in a box wrapped in a bow waiting for you. But He has other gifts, too.

The gift of patience. The gift of perseverance. The gift of faith. All these things you can receive as you go through a difficult time. These are not tangible gifts but are still much-needed gifts, especially when you're feeling down.

God knows all the things you need—from the physical to the spiritual—and He wants you to receive them.

Ask for what you need and see what good gifts God wants to give you.

MATTHEW 10:30

And even the very hairs of your head are all numbered.

Oh great, God counts my hair. How is numbered hair encouraging?

People who love football know all kinds of useless trivia about the game—the number of left-handed catches by right-handed receivers, the number of times Peyton Manning says "Idaho" in a game, names of all the water boys at Super Bowl XXXIX . . . If a person finds the mundane trivia interesting, they really love the game.

Jesus pointed out the most mundane calculation of our life and said that God is even interested in that. It's one fact about someone you probably could not care less about. An average person has 100,000 hair follicles. God has each one numbered.

If He has the hairs on your head counted, then He knows when your left eye hurts. He knows the toenail on your third toe is infected. He knows you have cancer.

If He has the hairs on your head counted, then He must know what you need, when you need it, and how to get it to you.

If God knows all your trivia, then He must be passionate about you.

MATTHEW 11:28–30

Come to me, all you who are weary and burdened, and I will give you rest. Take my yoke upon you and learn from me, for I am gentle and humble in heart, and you will find rest for your souls. For my yoke is easy and my burden is light.

"Thanks, I've got it." The most prideful, damaging statement we can make at times.

Think of a person trying to maneuver a couch down three flights of stairs. A sofa bed no less. In a dark stairwell. Late at night. "I've got it." Why deny help when others are offering to step in and help carry the load? It doesn't make any sense.

But we do that with God. God offers to carry the burden and we pridefully wave Him off. "I can do this, thanks." What are you afraid of? God will see you as weak? Others will see you as weak? People will think you can't handle responsibility?

You are weak. Admit it. The responsible thing to do is to ask for help.

You don't have to carry the burden by yourself. You can get through the issues of life if you just allow God to help.

Once you give it to God, life gets much easier.

49

MARK 6:50–51

Immediately he spoke to them and said, "Take courage! It is I. Don't be afraid." Then he climbed into the boat with them, and the wind died down. They were completely amazed. . . .

When we're in a storm, where is Jesus?

He doesn't call from the safety of dry land, waving a flashlight or semaphore flags. "Get to the shore fast!"

He doesn't pull up alongside in a National Guard rescue ship. "You okay?"

He doesn't send a text message from heaven. "Praying for you . . ."

Jesus climbs into your boat when the storms hit and stays with you until the wind dies down. Wherever the worst place could be, Jesus is not afraid to get onboard. And He sticks with you during the storm. Jesus doesn't always take away the storm; no promises there. But by His actions, He does promise to stay with you during the storm.

Storms will happen, but you don't have to face them alone. Jesus will go along with you for the ride.

LUKE 18:27

But He said, "The things which are impossible with men are possible with God." (NKJV)

When Jesus made this statement, He was talking about rich people getting saved and having a relationship with God. How does that apply to you right now?

It may seem impossible that a rich person could ever see their need for God. With all their needs met on earth, why would they ever turn their heart to heaven? Impossible change of heart? Not when you involve God in the equation.

This verse confirms that God can do the impossible, but that doesn't mean all things are probable. If there's an impossible outcome, God gets the glory. If things fall apart, man is to blame. The stubbornness of man's will thwarts the impossible every time. That doesn't deter or intimidate God at all. He has other means and better plans in the works.

We should never say "God can't."

We should always remember *God can*.

JOHN 14:1

Do not let your hearts be troubled. You believe in God; believe also in me.

Belief in Jesus Christ gives you the ultimate comfort.

Company fires you. "I trust in Jesus."

Spouse wants out of the marriage. "But I know Jesus loves me."

Enemies attack you. "Okay, but Jesus is on my side."

Death hits your family. "Thankfully Jesus is with us."

Doctor has bad news. "Jesus will never leave me."

No bad news can overwhelm or discount or destroy the fact that Jesus loves you, that God wants a relationship with you, and that He promises to be with you always.

What's the trouble if you know Jesus?

JOHN 14:26

> But the Advocate, the Holy Spirit, whom the Father will send in my name, will teach you all things and will remind you of everything I have said to you.

The word for *Advocate* in the Greek is *paraklētos*. The word has a number of translations.

It can mean a person who comes to your assistance in a time of need.

A person who pleads your case for you, like in court.

Or simply a guide.

When we see someone in court with their lawyer, the lawyer leans over at times to the client, suggesting, encouraging, and warning. That's what the Holy Spirit does. He's our Public Defender.

During hard times, the Holy Spirit is teaching you and reminding you. He's teaching you how to love God more and showing you biblical truths. He's reminding you that God loves you and Jesus died for you.

All you have to do is listen, agree, and obey.

You're not alone during your struggle. Your Advocate is right by your side.

53

JOHN 14:27

Peace I leave with you; my peace I give to you. Not as the world gives do I give to you. Let not your hearts be troubled, neither let them be afraid. (ESV)

Earthly peace just isn't working out as you hoped. When we seek peace, we want the absence of conflict. No drama. No ruffled feathers. Just leave me alone and stop bothering me.

But life can't just leave you alone. There's always something . . . from the weather, to the car, to the kids. Homework, housework, work work. Demands everywhere you go.

Even vacations are stressful. Packing, traveling, parking, unpacking, sightseeing, crowds, expenses, packing again, unpacking again.

What you need is a different kind of peace—a supernatural peace. The world can't understand it. The world says "stop whining" and "pick yourself up." The world says "get a grip" and "get over it."

Jesus says "Don't worry, I've got this. Trust in me. It'll all work out because I said it will all work out." Jesus changes our expectation and turns our focus from the world to heaven. We see events and problems as He sees them, and we relax. From heaven, things don't look so bad. And besides, God is in control.

Jesus leaves you with peace. He gives it to you. Take it and enjoy.

JOHN 15:11

I have told you this so that my joy may be in you and that your joy may be complete.

God wants you to have complete joy, not partial joy. Not a sliver of happiness or a dollop of bliss. He wants you to have complete joy.

We think joy is like a puzzle, where we have to fit together the pieces of our lives just perfectly, doing all the right things in perfect alignment. However, there's always this one piece missing. We stress out. We frantically search everywhere. We need that lost piece or we can't have joy!

Jesus hands us a complete and final picture of that joy, not pieces and parts. The whole enchilada.

So what did He just tell His disciples in John 15 so that their joy could be complete? Previous to this verse, Jesus laid out the picture of vines and branches. He is the vine and we are the branches. We have to remain in Him so we can bear much fruit. He went on to make sure they understood that as the Father loved Him, He loved them.

The key bit of information for complete joy was connection, relationship, and love. Stay close to God and you'll see the perfect picture of joy.

55

JOHN 15:13

Greater love has no one than this, than to lay down one's
life for his friends. (NKJV)

"The Greatest Love of All" was a mega-hit for Whitney
Houston. The song resonated with people. It was frequently sung at weddings and funerals. It showed people's passion to explore and understand that great love.

The lyrics to that song say that the greatest love of all is found
inside of oneself. But in John 15:13 Jesus explained where that
love can really be found.

Not in one's heart, but in one's sacrifice.

If you find sacrifice, you will find great love. If someone says,
"I'll lay down my life for you," that's great love. If someone
refuses to budge or give up anything for you, that's not great
love. It's not even good love. It's just convenience or self-love.

You are loved. Jesus proved that. He laid down His life for
you. He set the example of perfect love. He showed His love.
He didn't just talk about it.

You won't find any greater love at all in this world, but you can
show it by laying down your life for others as Jesus did for you.

JOHN 15:15

No longer do I call you servants, for a servant does not know what his master is doing; but I have called you friends, for all things that I heard from My Father I have made known to you. (NKJV)

You've got a friend.

James Taylor sang it, but Jesus showed it.

We think God is the chess player and we are the pawns. He's the boss and we're the workers.

Jesus doesn't see you that way. He calls us BFFs—Best Friends Forever, emphasis on the *forever*. He doesn't keep secrets from you, like a boss would keep from his employees. He's happy to pass along any information from His dad.

If we are not servants, then our relationship with Him is not based on service or total hours clocked in or even the quality of our performance. Our relationship is based on love and acceptance.

Friends don't fill out performance reviews or receive paychecks for hours spent doing their job. Jesus calls you friend because He loves you for being you.

JOHN 16:33

I have said these things to you, that in me you may have peace. In the world you will have tribulation. But take heart; I have overcome the world. (ESV)

Take heart. What does that mean?

The Greek word used there is *tharseō*. The word means to have courage and be of good cheer. Cheerful courage.

Jesus just pointed to himself in John 16:33 as the only way to find peace in this world. He acknowledged that life would not be trouble free, but we should know that He had overcome the world.

So we don't have to worry. Jesus has everything under control. We can relax. He'll fight our problems.

If you don't have to worry, then you can have courage. If Jesus is taking care of you, then be cheerful. Cheerful courage. Happy strength. Joyful peace.

Jesus doesn't ask you to *like* this sentiment. He tells you to *know* it. When you know it, it'll change your attitude. Problems . . . no big deal. Hardships . . . laugh in their face.

You can't overcome the world, but you know the One who has.

ROMANS 5:3–4

Not only that, but we rejoice in our sufferings, knowing that suffering produces endurance, and endurance
produces character, and character produces hope. (ESV)

We think that suffering does us no good. That hard times have no reason or meaning. That's not true. Our suffering does us some good. It builds character. Suffering forces us to look to outside means of support. When our world comes crashing down around us, we realize we can't trust the world to sustain us. Our usual means of comfort and routine don't work. We must turn to God.

We get through the hard times with His help, waiting patiently for relief. We learn perseverance in the process.

As our trust and endurance grow, so does our character, revealing the fruits of the Spirit—love, joy, peace, patience, kindness, goodness, faithfulness, gentleness, and self-control.

Then, as our perseverance builds and our character strengthens, we realize we can get through anything with God's help. We begin to hope and do not see our problems as a dead end but rather an opportunity to grow personally and relationally with God.

You can't avoid suffering, but you can use it to make you a better follower of God.

59

ROMANS 8:15

For you have not received a spirit of slavery leading to fear again, but you have received a spirit of adoption as sons by which we cry out, "Abba! Father!" (NASB)

D on't be afraid. You're family.

What makes you "family"? In our world, blood. Heritages share common DNA and genetic traits passed on from generation to generation. Marriage unites families, brought together by commitment.

Paul said in Romans that we have the Holy Spirit inside us, and that Holy Spirit makes us a part of a family. It's not based on blood, but it is based on commitment . . . commitment to Jesus Christ.

We share one common Father, too. You're not the great-great-great-great-grandchild of God. You are His child, first generation, adopted into His family. You can call Him Dad.

Your family may disappoint you on earth. But your heavenly Daddy won't. You're not His slave or His hired worker . . . you are His child.

ROMANS 8:28

And we know that God causes all things to work together for good to those who love God, to those who are called according to His purpose. (NASB)

Whatever "thing" you are going through, God is working to help you come out of it.

From where you stand right now, that may be hard to believe, but it's true: God is working. The "good thing" has not been realized. It's coming. Don't miss it.

You can miss the "good thing" God is doing if you don't love Him and you reject His calling.

But if you love God, then you know He loves you. So when you're going through a "bad thing," you know God has not left you. You know He is working. You know everything happens with purpose. You know He has called you to discover that purpose.

Through all things—good and bad—there is a good being worked out. Not all things will be good. Some things will be harder and very difficult. But if you love God, then you know good things are coming.

61

ROMANS 8:31

What then shall we say to these things? If God is for us, who can be against us? (ESV)

If God is for you, on your side, cheering you on, what opponent could possibly overcome Him?

We want life to be like a blowout in sports. A blowout occurs when one team scores in the opening seconds and continues to pound the opponents with more points, blocking the opponents from ever scoring. 48–0. 76–0. 102–0.

Life isn't like that. We face forces that push back and get ahead at times. We'll score big in a relationship, then lose a job. Or we'll ace our exam, only to have our car stolen. We'll see a prayer answered, then get bad news from the doctor. During those times we want to think God has lost His edge, that the enemy found His weakness and we're doomed to lose.

As long as we live on earth, the score will go up and down. All God promises is that at the final buzzer, all those who believe in Him will win. It might seem like a close game, but it's not. No matter how difficult life may have been, a believer in Christ will stand in the winner's circle with Jesus, holding His hand high.

You will win because God is eternally for you.

62

ROMANS 8:34

Who is he who condemns? It is Christ who died, and furthermore is also risen, who is even at the right hand of God, who also makes intercession for us. (NKJV)

Sitting in court by yourself before a judge can be intimidating. Walking into the IRS office without anyone by your side can be scary. Facing a Senate committee and hours of grueling questions can be a nightmare.

We don't like courts, the IRS offices, or a Senate committee because we're afraid of being condemned and blamed for something we did or didn't do. In situations like that, we want to have someone by our side.

The best person to have at our side is an expert. Having a pet dog by your side may offer some comfort, but even Fido slips under the desk when the senator from New York starts firing accusations.

Jesus intercedes for us when it comes to our guilt and sin. He's an expert in that field, because, as God, He knows what's holy and what's not. He came to die for us and fulfill the law's requirements for the death penalty. He knows His stuff.

Jesus intercedes and does not condemn. When the accusations fly, Jesus reminds the court, "I paid the price for that one. Not guilty."

ROMANS 8:37

No, in all these things we are more than conquerors through him who loved us. (ESV)

Love conquers all? Apparently.
Since God loves us, He conquered hate.
Since God knows the future, He conquered time.
Since God is the ultimate power, He conquered all enemies.
Since God died for us, He conquered sin.

A conqueror moves into enemy territory, defeats the enemy, renders them powerless, then takes over the place where that enemy once ruled.

God invites us as His followers to join Him in His conquest.

As a result, we are more than conquerors. More? What more could we possibly need or want?

The "more" is more than we could imagine. It's not just about defeat, but victory, now and forever. It's not just about taking over, but freeing the captives and allowing the prisoners to escape bondage.

God's love conquers everything, and He finds new ways to surprise us.

ROMANS 8:38–39

For I am convinced that neither death nor life, neither angels nor demons, neither the present nor the future, nor any powers, neither height nor depth, nor anything else in all creation, will be able to separate us from the love of God that is in Christ Jesus our Lord.

Nothing can separate you from the love of God.

Is that true?

Everything described in this verse is from the outside, trying to convince you on the inside that God doesn't love you. Death says God is powerless. Life is hard so God must be punishing you. Demons whisper lies. The future may look bleak so apparently God has given up on you. And on and on . . .

Those suggestions can do you no harm unless you accept them.

The only place to look to find confirmation of God's love for you is Christ Jesus. He showed God's love, spoke about it, and sacrificed to prove it. Sometimes these outside forces reveal God's love to you, but they can be inconsistent. Jesus' love never wavers. There's no doubt about it.

So no matter what life throws at you, don't look anywhere else to find the proof of God's love except in Jesus Christ.

ROMANS 15:13

May the God of hope fill you with all joy and peace as you trust in him, so that you may overflow with hope by the power of the Holy Spirit.

We run our lives on empty just like we drive around in our cars. We flirt with disaster wondering how much we can squeeze out of that fuel indicator light. Is it twenty miles? Maybe thirty. Let's see if we can get to the next exit . . . forty miles down the road.

Later, as we sit on the side of the road waiting for the tow truck, we wonder why we didn't fill up. What made us push to empty? Usually it's pride. We thought we could do it ourselves.

Living close to empty only causes us worry as we stare at the fuel indicator. We forget to look at the speedometer or even out the window. If we fill up, it's one less thing to worry about.

God wants to fill our tanks, not with distractions and sermons, but with joy, peace, and hope. Where do we get that kind of fuel? At a gas station named Trust. As you pull up into that station, you tell the attendant to "fill 'er up." The fuel flows freely, pouring over and spilling on the ground. "So much joy, peace, and hope," you say. "We have plenty where that came from," the attendant says with a smile.

Trust God and let your tank overflow.

1 CORINTHIANS 14:33

For God is not the author of confusion but of peace, as in all the churches of the saints. (NKJV)

If you're lost and confused, unable to make heads or tails of the situation, trying to find your way out of a dark tunnel with no idea where the exit is . . . that's not God's fault.

If things are spinning out of control, falling apart and there's no order in the court . . . don't blame God.

God is not about confusion and disorder. He makes sense. He's clear as day. He is light. He is the way. You can't get lost with God.

Confusion is not from God. Nor is chaos. Those things happen when a person looks somewhere besides God, making detours that made sense at the time but eventually led nowhere.

If things are chaotic in your world, it's because you're trying to do things by your own effort. You trust only yourself to get it done. You may be working with a group of people but soon learn that they all have their own compasses, pointing in different directions.

Make God your true north. Use Him as a flashlight in darkness. Follow His straight path to righteousness. Everything makes sense to God. He's at peace and wants you to join Him.

2 CORINTHIANS 1:3-4

Praise be to the God and Father of our Lord Jesus Christ,
the Father of compassion and the God of all comfort,
who comforts us in all our troubles, so that we can comfort those in any trouble with the comfort we ourselves
receive from God.

If you've experienced any comfort in your life, it could only
come from God.

The enemy (the world, too) doesn't want you to experience true comfort. So it offers a false sense of comfort through
physical pleasure, monetary success, and job security. However,
when those things fail, we realize they weren't as trustworthy
as we thought.

True comfort draws you closer to God. You understand He
has the power. You know you are accepted and loved. You are
convinced that everything will be all right.

But that comfort doesn't stop with you.

When we have experienced that comfort, we are likely to tell
others who are troubled. We explain to them how to find rest
in God. We direct them to the loving arms of God.

God can comfort any trouble experienced by anyone at any
time. He's the God of all comfort, and He wants you to relax
and trust Him.

Then go and comfort others.

2 CORINTHIANS 4:8–9

We are hard-pressed on every side, yet not crushed; we are perplexed, but not in despair; persecuted, but not forsaken; struck down, but not destroyed. (NKJV)

No matter how bad it seems, how surrounded you feel on all sides, how overwhelmed and inundated your situation has become . . . it's not over.

Paul felt that in his ministry. Opposition constantly hammered his efforts to reach people for Christ. That didn't mean it was all over.

You can take a two-by-four to a car and smash out all the windows and headlights, and dent every inch of the hood and side panels, and the car will still drive. It'll look terrible, but it will get you places.

If you're beat up, don't give up. If you're struck down, don't stay down. It may look bad, but it's not hopeless.

God paid the price for beaten lives. He's in the restoration business.

2 CORINTHIANS 4:16

So we do not lose heart. Though our outer self is wasting away, our inner self is being renewed day by day. (ESV)

One look in the mirror every day confirms this verse. We are wasting away.

Sags, bags, wrinkles, and rashes prove our outward condition. Nobody is getting younger.

Many defy that truth and try with technology and medical advances to reverse the aging process. It may work for a little while. But in the end, time wins.

Just because our outside wastes away doesn't mean the inside has to. In fact, inwardly we can renew and grow stronger, with a fresh perspective on life. We can't control our aging livers or sagging earlobes, but we can control our heart, soul, mind, and strength. By injecting those areas with healthy doses of Scripture and covering our internal workings with a prescription of prayer, we can get a new inside every day.

Sure, our bodies are deteriorating, but that's only for a short time. Once resurrected, we will live at the perfect age, with indestructible bodies. For now, let's work on the inside, which will last forever.

2 CORINTHIANS 4:17

For our light and momentary troubles are achieving for
us an eternal glory that far outweighs them all.

You may not call your troubles right now "light" and "momentary," but they are.

When we see our troubles compared with others', they don't seem so heavy. We also have a God who asks us to come to Him with our burdens and He will give us rest.

Our troubles won't last forever. They may last a day or a few years, but with an eternal perspective, they are only a moment—the equivalent of one second when we use an eternal calendar.

We must also see those troubles as achieving something greater—an eternal glory. Those troubles introduce people to God's love and strength. Outsiders watch a Christian's reaction to troubles and understand true faith.

The temporary is achieving the eternal. It's tough now. It'll be glorious later.

2 CORINTHIANS 4:18

So we fix our eyes not on what is seen, but on what is unseen, since what is seen is temporary, but what is unseen is eternal.

D on't look at what you see. A strange request from Paul the apostle. We have eyes made to see moving objects within our field of vision. It's only natural to fix our eyes on what we see.

The key word Paul uses is *fix*. Fixing our eyes means to stare at, fixate on, and dwell upon. If we only trust what we see, then we will be overwhelmed. We have to look beyond what we see.

Instead of focusing on our troubles, we must focus our heart on the unseen—God and His ways and purposes.

So what's going on in the unseen? God is influencing hearts. He's moving people around. He's whispering new thoughts in ears. He's changing policies and invading countries.

We may never see those things happen in our lifetime, so we see with faith, trusting the unseen and the work God is doing there.

Seeing is not believing. Not seeing and still trusting is believing.

2 CORINTHIANS 5:17

Therefore, if anyone is in Christ, the new creation has
come: The old has gone, the new is here!

Commercials always try to sell a new you.
That old car . . . toss it. You need a new you!
That old food you were eating . . . gag me. You need
a new you!

That old antiperspirant you used . . . how did you ever have
any friends? You need a new you.

Infomercials pound that idea into you for thirty minutes.
Insane workout programs show what a new you can look like.
Fat, unhappy, unsatisfied you versus thin, confident, and satis-
fied you.

Jesus should put out an infomercial. Before Jesus—lost, confused, unfulfilled. After Jesus—joyful, assured, and forgiven.
What a transformation! And it can all be yours . . . for free,
because Jesus paid the price.

The difference is that the new car will be old one day, a new
antiperspirant will hit the shelves, and these bodies will eventually fall apart no matter how hard we try, but salvation that
comes from Jesus is new every morning.

The new you is forever new and never grows old.

GALATIANS 5:1

For freedom Christ has set us free; stand firm therefore, and do not submit again to a yoke of slavery. (ESV)

Why did Christ come to this earth, die on the cross, and resurrect from the dead?

For our freedom.

His teaching sets us free from the lies of this world.

His death sets us free from the penalty of sin.

His resurrection sets us free from the fear of death.

You were meant to be free. Take off the chains and walk out of your cell. Christ set you free!

Yet many remain behind bars by choice. They know they can be free but prefer slavery. Why? They are more afraid of freedom than imprisonment. The sinful life is comfortable and knowable. When they hear Christ's offer, they say "Freedom . . . true freedom . . . what is that? What's required of me? What's the catch?"

The catch . . . Give your life to God and let Him remove the shackles. Be a servant to God, who knows what's best for you—freedom.

GALATIANS 6:9

And let us not grow weary of doing good, for in due season
we will reap, if we do not give up. (ESV)

Impatient farmers are the worst farmers.

What if they planted the seeds, then went out the next
day and thought, *This is dumb. Nothing but a bunch of dry
seeds in the ground.* Maybe in their frustration they dug it all
up and decided to start over again.

You would say to the farmer, "Give it time. In the next few
months it will be a harvest of good food."

What if the weather was harsh one year and the crops were
lost; would you tell the farmer to get out of the business? Bad
years happen. It's still no reason to give up.

In our lives we hit rough patches and we don't see fruit from
all our efforts. Is that a reason to give up? Like the farmer, we
must stay the course, keep trusting, and wait patiently.

Doing good—doing the right thing—isn't always easy. You
cannot give up when bad things happen. Things are just starting to take root, sprout, and break ground.

Be patient and don't give up.

EPHESIANS 1:18

I pray that the eyes of your heart may be enlightened, so that you will know what is the hope of His calling, what are the riches of the glory of His inheritance in the saints. (NASB)

Hope lights up the heart.

Hope gives you something to look forward to. It helps you see beyond the bad and get a glimpse of the good. Hope pushes you forward when life pushes back.

A Christian's hope is in the future. He has so much to look forward to—a glorious inheritance, an everlasting reunion. It's an abundance that will take eternity to process and enjoy.

Your heart needs to see that. Your mind needs to know that. Your spirit needs to embrace that.

When all three areas of your life—heart, mind, spirit—look forward to the eternal relationship God promises you, you will have hope and anticipation.

EPHESIANS 2:4–5

But because of his great love for us, God, who is rich in mercy, made us alive with Christ even when we were dead in transgressions—it is by grace you have been saved.

Dead people aren't rich. In fact, they really have nothing of any value.

Someone dead in their sins has even less. Not only do they have nothing, they have debt. The debt of their sins puts a negative value to their zero balance.

Those in Christ who are dead are very much alive. They have something . . . actually everything. Everything they could ever want. Everything they need for all eternity. They have a relationship with God given to them by God's grace and mercy. That love relationship saves them from nothingness. They have abundant life.

If you die and have God's love, mercy, life, grace, and salvation, you are richer than any person living on earth. You get to cash in on Christ's Life Assurance plan and enjoy those riches forever.

PHILIPPIANS 2:1–2

So if there is any encouragement in Christ, any comfort from love, any participation in the Spirit, any affection and sympathy, complete my joy by being of the same mind, having the same love, being in full accord and of one mind. (ESV)

If you are united in Christ, be comforted. You share the Holy Spirit with others.

That connection to God filters tenderness and compassion into your life. God is tender with you and compassionate about your relationship. He wants you to be tender and compassionate with others, too.

If God loves you and, in addition, everyone you know is loving to one another, your joy is complete because you are like-minded in every relationship you have in heaven and on earth.

There is joy in unity—being united with Christ . . . being united with those Christ loves. Division destroys your joy because you ruin the unity.

When one or more people gather together with like-mindedness and joy, it's actually called a party!

PHILIPPIANS 3:12

Not that I have already obtained all this, or have already arrived at my goal, but I press on to take hold of that for which Christ Jesus took hold of me.

Press on.
Maybe you haven't gotten all that you wanted out of life, but press on.

Maybe you haven't arrived yet, but press on.

Christ has something for you to take on as you press on. He's already obtained it for you, outlined it for you, designated it for you, but you need to receive it for yourself.

Success isn't arriving at the goal. Even with all that Paul accomplished late in his life, he still didn't feel he had crossed the finish line. We're never really finished serving God. Success is being focused on the goal and moving toward it.

When will that happen? When will you cross the line and obtain the prize? When you die. The race is officially over at that time.

So press on, accomplishing everything God wants you to do in the meantime. Cross the finish line knowing you gave it all that you had.

PHILIPPIANS 4:6

Do not be anxious about anything, but in every situation, by prayer and petition, with thanksgiving, present your requests to God.

D on't worry.
About anything.
Worry, many feel, is their duty when hit with stress. They think that by worrying they are doing something and are therefore engaged in the solution. Worry solves nothing; it only makes things worse for yourself.

Philippians 4:6 says don't worry . . . pray. Present your need before God and leave it there. If you went to valet parking and left your car with the attendant but worried about it all during dinner, you would have a terrible time. You are saying you don't trust the attendant, and that the car was more important than dinner.

When stressed, we need to leave our worries with God and walk away. If we worry, we're saying that we don't trust God with the keys to our lives. We lose appreciation for what else He's given us. We think He doesn't hear us or care.

Worry solves nothing. Presenting your need to God and leaving it there for Him to handle solves everything.

PHILIPPIANS 4:7

And the peace of God, which surpasses all understanding,
will guard your hearts and minds through Christ Jesus.
(NKJV)

You can't really understand God's peace.
    It's a peace unlike anything else you can find on this
earth.

It's a transcendental peace, not the meditation kind that
hypnotizes you to think there's no suffering going on in the
world, but it supersedes . . . exceeds . . . transcends all worldly
efforts to find a solution to peace.

There is no promise in the Bible that God will make this earth
peaceful. There will always be struggles in the world.

God does give us a solution to the struggles by allowing us to
feel that peace inside us in the midst of all struggles. The peace
is in our heart and in our mind, not in the world.

We are guarded by God because we have faith, trusting Him
to take care of us. We put aside the worry and the heartache.
We know it will all work out in the end.

You don't have to understand the troubles in this world. Just
understand that God loves you, He's working around you, and
He's helping you get through this. That's peace, man.

81

PHILIPPIANS 4:12

I know what it is to be in need, and I know what it is to have plenty. I have learned the secret of being content in any and every situation, whether well fed or hungry, whether living in plenty or in want.

What's the secret of being content when you're well fed? Don't want more and more.

What's the secret of being content when you're hungry? Be thankful for what you have.

What's the secret of being content when living in plenty? Give to others.

What's the secret of being content when living in want? Desire God over everything else.

These secrets to life show that living with much or little is not very different. Both have their challenges. Greed affects the rich and the poor. Gluttony challenges the starving and the satisfied.

The secret is always to be thankful for what you have and to give to others no matter how much—or little—you have.

By looking to Jesus Christ we see someone who had everything in heaven and gave it all up to live poorly on earth for us. The entire time here Jesus gave everything He had, thanking His Father for the opportunity to bless others.

PHILIPPIANS 4:13

I can do all this through him who gives me strength.

The Greek word for "all this" or "all things" is *pas*. It means all, any, each, everyone, everything. Pretty much ALL things.

Whatever you are going through, you can do all you need to do because Christ gives you strength.

You don't have to grow weary. God will carry you through it.

You don't have to grow weak. God can lift you on His shoulders.

You can't do it by yourself. Don't try. You don't have the energy, the stamina, or the foresight to make the right choices.

Lean on God . . . better yet, surrender yourself totally in His arms.

He's got you. He's got the power.

PHILIPPIANS 4:19

And my God will meet all your needs according to the
riches of his glory in Christ Jesus.

We love the first part of this verse—God will meet all
your needs. That's great news. But how?

The verse goes on and says all our needs will be
met according to the riches of His glory in Christ Jesus.

Our needs are not met by our riches. They are met by His
riches.

Our needs are not met by our glory. They are met by His glory.

So the real question is what do we really need that Jesus Christ
provides? We need a relationship with God. We need forgiveness. We need the promise of eternal life. We need guidance
on how to live sacrificially. We need hope and a second chance.

Jesus Christ provided all of that through His sacrifice on
the cross.

You are rich. You have everything you really need in Him.
What more could you want?

COLOSSIANS 3:2

Set your minds on things that are above, not on things that are on earth. (ESV)

It's easy to be frustrated by this world. It's what we see. It presents itself to us all the time on the news, on social media posts, and in conversation. What we constantly see influences our mood. It tempts our decisions. We are bombarded with the world.

Paul said to the Colossians, "Don't focus on it." Of course we'll see the world and hear all about it, but we don't have to dwell on it.

Don't focus on the earthly; look to the heavenly. Something terrible happens here on earth; look to heaven for the wonderful. Confused on earth . . . look to heaven for clarity. Hopeless here . . . look up there. Bad news . . . see the good news.

This world is discouraging. But you don't have to fix your mind on it. You can choose where your attention ultimately will dwell.

Set your mind on God in heaven. The view is much better from there.

1 THESSALONIANS 4:17–18

Then we who are alive, who are left, will be caught up together with them in the clouds to meet the Lord in the air, and so we will always be with the Lord. Therefore encourage one another with these words. (ESV)

Jesus is coming!

When He does come, everyone alive at the time immediately transports to be with Him forever. Those in the graves rise up, resurrected, to join everyone else. This world will all be a distant memory from our past. Everything changes in the blink of the eye.

Until then, we should be encouraged by those words. Why? The return of Jesus Christ tells us that it's not always going to be like this. This life is only a season, an appetizer, a trailer for the big feature. God can change time faster than you can snap your fingers. Hope is coming.

Everyone will experience this moment—alive or dead. Whatever troubled us won't matter. Our problems will go away. All debts gone. Only one relationship will matter. Our relationship with Jesus Christ.

This life is not forever. Jesus Christ is coming to take you away to the next.

Be encouraged by this truth.

1 TIMOTHY 6:12

Fight the good fight of the faith. Take hold of the eternal life to which you were called when you made your good confession in the presence of many witnesses.

There are good fights and there are bad fights.

A bad fight is ego-driven. Someone wants to be right or gain more power. A bad fight can be based on misunderstanding or ignorance. In bad fights, people get hurt, some severely. Grudges begin. Forgiveness ends.

A good fight is God-driven. It's all about getting the message of God's love into the world. The fight occurs because God is right and He holds all the power. There's no misunderstanding because a good fight is based on truth, supported by faith.

A good fighter takes hold of their eternal life and heads into battle. There's no fear of death because the good fighter is assured of their future. He stands up before others and confesses his faith and speaks the truth. People scream at and demean a good fighter, attacking reputations and sanity. The good fighter doesn't mind. He's standing up for a truly good God who stood up for him when He allowed himself to be nailed to a cross.

Jesus fought the good fight and won. Keep fighting the right fights and God will raise your hand in victory.

2 TIMOTHY 1:7

For the Spirit God gave us does not make us timid, but gives us power, love and self-discipline.

If you believe in Jesus Christ, you have the Holy Spirit in you.
If you have the Holy Spirit in you, there's no reason to whine, complain, or wonder, *How am I ever going to get through this?*

When Popeye needed strength, he popped open a can of spinach. Miraculously, his muscles expanded and his courage exploded. Popeye was then able to physically conquer anything in his way.

The same is true spiritually for those with the Spirit of God.

Confronting a fierce enemy, believers have an inner power. Battling hate, believers have a supernatural love. Facing temptation, believers have spiritual self-discipline.

With the Holy Spirit inside you, you are strong, filled with love, and able to live a disciplined life.

Don't forget what's inside you. Pop open a can of Holy Spirit and take on the world.

HEBREWS 3:13

But encourage one another daily, as long as it is called "Today," so that none of you may be hardened by sin's deceitfulness.

Encouragement is a group effort. We must cheer each other on.

Sin continues to deceive people into thinking there is no hope and things are falling apart. Sin hardens our consciences. We think we're all doomed and evil will win once again.

Every day we need fresh encouragement because every day evil releases a new message of despair. We cannot miss a day without being encouraged or giving encouragement.

Today's encouragement may help tomorrow, but a fresh batch of discouragement works quickly to erase our memories.

So do your part and spread encouragement. Tell others you are praying for them. Send them a text saying you're thinking about them. Tell a joke. Visit a friend in the hospital.

As you encourage, you are encouraged. One day your supply of encouragement will run out and a friend will be there to fill you up.

HEBREWS 4:15

For we do not have a high priest who is unable to empathize with our weaknesses, but we have one who has been tempted in every way, just as we are—yet he did not sin.

High priests seem so . . . high. Their job title screams separation from the people they serve. Try talking to a senior pastor of a ten-thousand-member church. You have to go through three secretaries just to get on their schedule for a meeting in six months.

So when we have problems, does our High Priest, Jesus Christ, have time for us, or do we need to get on His schedule for next week?

Actually, He has plenty of time for you. He is so intimately aware of your situation that He even empathizes with you. Jesus knows the temptations you are facing because He faced those temptations, too. He left His busy schedule in heaven and came to earth just to experience our lives. He understands our weaknesses because He saw them firsthand.

Jesus mastered our lives and wants us to go to Him when we feel we've mangled our lives. He made time for us and continues to make time for us.

He's been there. He knows how it feels.

HEBREWS 4:16

Let us then with confidence draw near to the throne of
grace, that we may receive mercy and find grace to help
in time of need. (ESV)

Since we know the High Priest knows us and cares for us,
we can approach Him confidently.

That throne has an open-door policy. It doesn't need
to. As God (and King), He could put restrictions on who ap-
proaches Him. Maybe your giving record could come into question. Maybe your church attendance. Maybe only sinless people
can make an appearance with God face-to-face.

Thankfully not. That throne has a Grace Policy. God loves
everyone, despite what they've done. Everyone can come to God
to receive mercy, grace, and help in a time of need.

No restrictions. No hours of operation. He's not even off on
Sundays. God tells us to approach the throne and don't be shy.

Confidently draw near to God right now. He's been waiting
to hear from you. The throne is open.

HEBREWS 6:18

So that by two unchangeable things, in which it is impossible for God to lie, we who have fled for refuge might have strong encouragement to hold fast to the hope set before us. (ESV)

God can't lie. Hold on to this hope.

If He says He loves you, He loves you.

If He says He will never leave you or forsake you, believe it.

If He says nothing will separate you from His love, don't doubt it for one minute.

It's impossible for God to lie because there is nothing deceitful in Him. He has no reason to lie. The truth is too good. He doesn't need to cover His tracks because He's never done anything wrong. He doesn't need to impress anyone because He's God.

Whatever you are running from has probably lied to you. Whoever wants to take you down needed lies to justify his or her actions.

We live in a world where everything lies, so we assume God must lie, too. He can't. It's impossible.

Be encouraged that there is at least one thing in this world you can trust . . . always.

HEBREWS 10:24–25

And let us consider how to stir up one another to love
and good works, not neglecting to meet together, as is the
habit of some, but encouraging one another, and all the
more as you see the Day drawing near. (ESV)

W hatever trials you are facing, keep gathering around
other Christians. Stay close to the flock. Satan loves
to pick off the strays. Stray sheep are vulnerable and
defenseless.

Some give up on the flock because they don't see any benefit.
The benefit comes silently, through teaching, welcoming, eye
contact, conversations, corporate worship, all of which the Holy
Spirit uses to encourage you to love more and do more.

This verse also makes clear that we should not only receive
encouragement, but give it, too. Sometimes by encouraging
others we are encouraged. We find purpose and enjoy being
used to help others by doing good deeds.

Don't give up on being around other Christians. On that
future day, the return of Jesus Christ, we will all be together
for eternity. Get used to it now.

Stay . . . don't stray.

1 PETER 1:13

Therefore, preparing your minds for action, and being sober-minded, set your hope fully on the grace that will be brought to you at the revelation of Jesus Christ. (ESV)

Set your hope on the grace. How does that work?

If you put your hope on circumstances, circumstances will change and you'll be discouraged. If you put your hope in a person, that person changes their mind and you'll be confused.

Putting your hope in anything earthly only disappoints. This world cannot give any long-term, sustainable hope.

So with a fully alert and sober mind—not influenced by world events and fickle people—put your hope in God and specifically His grace.

His grace shows His complete acceptance of you and His willingness to receive you into His kingdom. Once you accept His invitation, your status cannot change. Nothing can separate you any longer from God. His grace is nonrefundable, nonexchangeable, never expires.

God wanted to make sure you understood this grace so much that He sent Jesus Christ to the earth to confirm it. So focus on grace and it won't disappoint you.

1 PETER 5:7

Cast all your anxiety on him because he cares for you.

All worries go directly to God.

The minute something starts to brew inside your head, constantly twisting around for a solution that it can't find, weaving in and out of real and make-believe, consuming your mind's time for hours . . . drop it off at God's inbox.

No, better yet, throw it in there as hard as you can. Give it a good, long cast like a fisherman releases his bait. A fisherman doesn't keep his hook close to him, right by his feet. He reels it out as far as it can go.

You want to separate yourself as far as you can from your anxieties. Drop them into God's deep waters and let Him fish it out and find a solution.

Why can you do this? Because He loves you. Because He knows you can't solve this on your own. God knows the solution; He just wants you to trust Him to get it done.

Cast away because He cares for you.

95

2 PETER 3:9

The Lord is not slow in keeping his promise, as some understand slowness. Instead he is patient with you, not wanting anyone to perish, but everyone to come to repentance.

There are days we think, *Jesus, please return today and make all things right.*

Then we think about the lost whose eternities would be set, and we hesitate. *No, Jesus, not today. So many would be separated from you.*

We think God moves too slowly, but He always has the bigger picture in mind, not only for our situation, but the lives of billions simultaneously. If He blessed you, He may have to cause hardship to someone else (someone loses their job so you can get their job). On the other hand, your hardship could be someone else's blessing.

Through it all, God is focused most on repentance. He doesn't want anyone to perish, living separated from Him in hell. He may be moving slowly in returning at the final trumpet call, meaning more pain and hardship for believers, but He's doing all He can to wring out the last few remaining souls who will believe.

In the meantime, our focus should be on the lost who are perishing. We pray that every moment more will come to believe in Him. A believer only faces temporary pain until Jesus returns, but when He does, so many will face eternal pain.

We must let Jesus take His time and continue to work on the hearts of people everywhere.

1 JOHN 1:9

If we confess our sins, He is faithful and just to forgive us
our sins and to cleanse us from all unrighteousness. (NKJV)

You can be forgiven.

Maybe the person you hurt won't forgive you. Maybe
those who defended the one you hurt won't forgive you.
It would be nice, but what you really need is God's forgiveness.

Others put you on trial and convict you in the courts of
their mind. It's not a fair trial since you can't defend yourself.
However, phone calls aren't answered and emails are ignored.
It's hard to ask forgiveness from people, and when you do,
they might not believe you are sincere. What can you do unless you try?

God puts everyone on trial for sin, and everyone is guilty.
The only way to escape punishment is to plead guilty and ask
for forgiveness. Jesus Christ provides that forgiveness by substituting His death for the death you deserve. You just have to
ask and your record will be clean.

Yes, seeking forgiveness from people is good, but seeking
forgiveness from God is best. He'll know your sincerity, and
He'll faithfully forgive. The punishment He offers is worse but
His forgiveness is best. And in the process, He'll help you find
reconciliation with others on earth.

1 JOHN 3:2

Beloved, we are God's children now, and what we will be has not yet appeared; but we know that when he appears we shall be like him, because we shall see him as he is. (ESV)

As much as we try not to, we grow up to be like our parents. We want to be independent, with our own identity, but our parents' influence on us is undeniable. We become like them.

That's what God is hoping by calling us children. He wants to influence us to become like our Father. We must watch Him, talk to Him, learn from Him so that He can build His character inside of us.

Jesus calls God His Father to help us understand this relationship. Jesus spoke about His own relationship with God, how He only did what His Father told him to do, how He glorified His Father in all that He did. We must do the same. In that sense, we will be like Jesus, followers of the same Father.

We are his children, and one day we will be in His presence, fully resurrected in our Father's house.

Home.

1 JOHN 4:4

Little children, you are from God and have overcome them, for he who is in you is greater than he who is in the world. (ESV)

God >World
Sometimes the formula doesn't quite seem that way. The world has a power and an influence that feels insurmountable. We feel like little children trying to battle the giants of this world.

But the Bible says the children of God need not worry. No more sleepless nights. No more checking under the bed. If you have God and He is your Father, then the world cannot overcome those who have a relationship with Him.

He's not far away. In fact, He's in you. While you are in the world, God is in you. If you carry around God in your heart, the greater One goes with you. The world cannot overcome you.

If God is in you, then You + Your Father > World.

It all adds up. Just know the formula works and don't feel helpless any longer.

1 JOHN 4:18

There is no fear in love, but perfect love casts out fear. For fear has to do with punishment, and whoever fears has not been perfected in love. (ESV)

You can't fear and love at the same time.

There are people in our lives who we find hard to love. If we trace that feeling to fear, we can understand a little better why. We're afraid to get close because they will only hurt us. We're afraid to move away or they will attack us. We're afraid to express emotions, dreams, and thoughts or we'll be ridiculed.

A perfect love has no fear. This kind of love has your best interests always in mind. It's a love that always protects, always hopes, always prays for you. This love never wants to hurt you unless it's for your benefit, not theirs. That kind of love makes you a more perfect person.

Can we find it on this earth? It's hard, and with humans it will always be flawed. But sometimes it's pretty amazing.

In heaven, we find the perfect lover—God. He doesn't want to control you. He doesn't want to make you into something you're not. He waits patiently for you and allows you to call the shots. He'd prefer that you stay close to His love because He knows that's the best place to be.

Don't try to find any other love on this earth until you've discovered this perfect love from Heaven. It will help you love better and make better choices over who to love.

REVELATION 21:4

And God will wipe away every tear from their eyes; there shall be no more death, nor sorrow, nor crying. There shall be no more pain, for the former things have passed away. (NKJV)

There are no tissues in heaven. No funerals or caskets. No Band-Aids or doctors. No chemotherapy or self-help books. No psychiatrists or counseling sessions. No grief support groups or group therapies. No aspirin. No toothaches. No sympathy cards. No relationship status changes. Nothing is lost. Nothing goes wrong.

Those things are in the world today, but one day that order of business will end. The earth's agenda will be torn to shreds. "That's not the way we do things anymore."

The new way will be about life and rejoicing. If there are tears, they will be tears of joy. As for pain . . . all gone. Sorry, doctors.

Imagine that world. God can't wait until you arrive, but in the meantime He's working things out, making sure as many people as possible will be there.

Anticipate that day and know it's coming as you go through the hard times. Right now won't be forever. Something much better is right around the corner.

SCRIPTURE LIST

1. Genesis 9:16
2. Genesis 21:6
3. Genesis 21:17
4. Genesis 22:17
5. Genesis 39:23
6. Genesis 50:20
7. Exodus 2:25
8. Exodus 3:8
9. Exodus 14:14
10. Exodus 14:19–20
11. Exodus 34:6–7
12. Numbers 6:24–26
13. Numbers 11:23
14. 2 Kings 6:17
15. 2 Chronicles 20:15
16. 2 Chronicles 32:7–8
17. Job 2:3
18. Job 2:6
19. Job 2:13
20. Job 6:8–9
21. Job 16:20–21
22. Psalm 10:17–18
23. Psalm 23:4
24. Psalm 27:1
25. Psalm 27:14
26. Psalm 46:1
27. Psalm 91:11–12
28. Psalm 121:7–8
29. Psalm 139:2–3
30. Psalm 145:18
31. Psalm 147:3
32. Proverbs 3:5–6
33. Proverbs 18:10
34. Isaiah 40:31
35. Isaiah 41:10
36. Jeremiah 29:11
37. Jeremiah 30:11
38. Habakkuk 3:19

39. Zephaniah 3:20
40. Zechariah 4:6
41. Matthew 5:4
42. Matthew 5:10
43. Matthew 6:25
44. Matthew 6:33
45. Matthew 6:34
46. Matthew 7:11
47. Matthew 10:30
48. Matthew 11:28–30
49. Mark 6:50–51
50. Luke 18:27
51. John 14:1
52. John 14:26
53. John 14:27
54. John 15:11
55. John 15:13
56. John 15:15
57. John 16:33
58. Romans 5:3–4
59. Romans 8:15
60. Romans 8:28
61. Romans 8:31
62. Romans 8:34
63. Romans 8:37
64. Romans 8:38–39
65. Romans 15:13
66. 1 Corinthians 14:33
67. 2 Corinthians 1:3–4
68. 2 Corinthians 4:8–9
69. 2 Corinthians 4:16
70. 2 Corinthians 4:17
71. 2 Corinthians 4:18
72. 2 Corinthians 5:17
73. Galatians 5:1
74. Galatians 6:9
75. Ephesians 1:18
76. Ephesians 2:4–5
77. Philippians 2:1–2
78. Philippians 3:12
79. Philippians 4:6
80. Philippians 4:7
81. Philippians 4:12
82. Philippians 4:13
83. Philippians 4:19
84. Colossians 3:2
85. 1 Thessalonians 4:17–18
86. 1 Timothy 6:12
87. 2 Timothy 1:7
88. Hebrews 3:13
89. Hebrews 4:15
90. Hebrews 4:16
91. Hebrews 6:18
92. Hebrews 10:24–25
93. 1 Peter 1:13
94. 1 Peter 5:7
95. 2 Peter 3:9
96. 1 John 1:9
97. 1 John 3:2
98. 1 John 4:4
99. 1 John 4:18
100. Revelation 21:4

TROY SCHMIDT is an author and television writer with credits at Disney, Nickelodeon, Tommy Nelson, and Lifeway. He has written for Max Lucado's HERMIE AND FRIENDS series and was the consulting producer for *The American Bible Challenge* with Jeff Foxworthy. His other book titles include *Saved, Release, 40 Days, Chapter by Chapter, In His Shoes: The Life of Jesus,* and many others. Troy has also written several children's books, including *Little Tree Found* and *Their Side of the Story.* He is a campus pastor at First Baptist Church of Windermere, Florida. Troy and his wife have three grown sons and make their home in Florida.

More from Troy Schmidt

Have you ever wanted to ask God what heaven is like? *The 100 Best Bible Verses on Heaven* goes straight to the source of all Truth to give insight into the afterlife. The 100 highlighted verses include well-known passages as well as hidden treasures. Each verse is followed by a brief devotional reading that will help you find understanding and comfort from the text, and in the process draw ever nearer to God.

The 100 Best Bible Verses on Heaven

How well do you know the great Bible verses on prayer? Whether we have memorized Scripture for years or have recently started reading the Bible, we have much to learn about prayer. Each verse is followed by a brief reading to explain the verse's significance and draw you nearer to God in prayer, making it perfect as a day-by-day devotional or as a starting point for further study.

The 100 Best Bible Verses on Prayer

❖BETHANYHOUSE

Stay up to date on your favorite books and authors with our free e-newsletters. Sign up today at bethanyhouse.com.

Find us on Facebook. facebook.com/BHPnonfiction

Follow us on Twitter. @bethany_house